Scripture quotations are taken from New International Version unless specified. Copyright © 1973, 1978, 1984 by International Bible Society, Colorado Springs, CO. 80921-3696

The Chaotic World of a Controller

Copyright © First Edition, 2007
Second Edition, 2016
By Carole McDuffee

Miracle House Publishing
P.O. Box 44814
Rio Rancho, New Mexico
87174-4814, U. S. A.

Printed in the United States of America. All rights reserved under international Copyright Law. Written permission must be secured from the author or publisher to use or reproduce any part of this book, except for brief quotations in critical reviews or articles.

Dedicated to my Lord and Savior, Jesus Christ, for the revelation He so willingly gives to set His people free. To my Precious Husband Gary, for always & without fail loving & supporting my endeavors. To my Dear Friend, Sandy Scott, (who has gone on to be with the Lord), for her

labor of love in editing this book!

Glory to God in the Highest!

Is not this the kind of fasting that I have chosen: to loose the chains of injustice and untie the cords of the yoke, to set the oppressed free and to break every yoke? And the yoke shall be destroyed because of the anointing (Isaiah 10:27).

For rebellion is as the sin of witchcraft (1 Samuel 15:23).

Table of Contents

Introduction..8

Chapter One

Family Dysfunction…The Highway to Unhealthy Control
....10

Chapter Two

The Trap of Control...14

Chapter Three

A Closer Look at the Insecure Heart......................25

Chapter Four

Multiplicity in the Valley of Control......................39

Chapter Five

Blatant Forms of Control..................................44

Chapter Six

Subtle Forms of Control...................................51

Chapter Seven

Are You a Victim of Control?.............................60

Chapter Eight

So I'm a Controller: What Do I Do Now?……………65

Chapter Nine

Sweet Surrender………………………………………….70

Scriptures to Aid You in Your Quest for Freedom from the Chaos of Controlling

Anxiety & Fear……………………………………….78
Trust…………………………………………………..84
Security……………………………………………….90
Healing………………………………………………..93

Endnotes……………………………………….99

Introduction

Many of us have grown up in dysfunctional homes. The American Medical Association estimates seventy-two percent of families are harboring someone who has an addiction, producing dysfunction.[1] Given such a high percentage, it is certain that there are untold numbers of individuals struggling with control, manipulation, and rebellion. According to the Bible, this is the sin of witchcraft (1 Samuel 15:23).

Like so many others, I grew up in a dysfunctional home environment. My father and my mother were both alcoholics and my mother was bipolar. To me, my home was normal. I didn't know at the time there is no such thing as a "normal" home. After all, how does one define "normal"? Because of the level of dysfunction in my home, I not only learned how to control others, I learned how to enable controllers. Caught up in a massive cycle of defeat that produced bouts of nervousness, anxiety, worry and frustration, my life became a world of chaos.

I give thanks to our gracious Heavenly Father, for as I began to call out to Him for answers, He quickly began to respond. He divulged many of the hows and whys of control. It is my hope and prayer that as you read this book, you will find freedom from control, whether you personally are the controller, or you are being victimized by one.

Though you are ultimately not responsible for those controllers in your life and their choices, you are responsible for yourself and the unhealthy habit of enabling them to control you or others close to you. In choosing to confront them, you will be taking a stand against this dysfunctional pattern in their lives. With prayer, this will disable their unhealthy behaviors and habits so they can be healed from the massive insecurities and fears they have developed as a result of growing up in an unstable home environment. You will be doing your part to guide them onto a path of life and freedom in Christ. Choosing to deal with your own choice to control, will also be life changing and powerful. Now, that's good fruit!

The truths within this book are not my own. It is to the glory of God that you hold this book in your hands. May the Lord richly bless you as you begin your journey to freedom in Christ from control.

Chapter One

Family Dysfunction…The Highway to Unhealthy Control

Family Dysfunction is much more rampant than many of us might imagine, and it almost always leads the way to unhealthy control.

Some experts say that 95% of families are dysfunctional in some magnitude. I am inclined to believe this is true, given the high percentage of alcohol and drug abuse, the wide variety of addictions, and the many forms of abuse blanketing a home where drug and alcohol abuse is prevalent.

The following statistics help to paint a lucid picture of dysfunction in our society. As I was doing my research for this book, I was moved inwardly by what I found. I think you will be also.

Though extreme, I began with a study the FBI did on thirty-six sexually motivated killers. Twenty-nine of the thirty-six had murdered multiple victims. Though many of us will never sexually abuse or murder someone, studying an extreme scenario paints a picture of dysfunction at its worst, thereby giving us a very distinct picture of dysfunction and its counterparts. Below are the percentages of dysfunction in the sexually motivated killer's homes:

1. 69% of their homes had alcohol abuse
2. 53% had psychiatric problems
3. 50% had criminal histories
4. 46% had sexual problems

Most of these individuals had trauma in some form of sexual or physical abuse, developmental failures stemming from trauma, and interpersonal failure on the part of caregivers to serve as positive role models for their children. [1]

A 2,000 US Census said that 60% of all American children come from divorced homes. [2] Jennifer Baker of the Forest Institute of Professional Psychology gave the percentages of divorce in first, second, and third marriages:

1. First marriage: 50%
2. Second marriages: 67%
3. Third marriages: 73% [3]

A counseling firm, Compass Interventions, gave these statistics:

1. 17.6 million people (1 in 12 adults) in the U. S. abuse alcohol.

2. 10 million abuse prescription drugs.

3. 6.5 million minors in the U. S. live with either an alcoholic mother or father.

4. 53% adults report someone in their family has a drinking problem. [4]

The American Medical Association says 72% of families have addictions. [5]

RAINN, (The Rape-Abuse-Incest National Network) says every 2 minutes someone is sexually assaulted. That is 213,000 victims of assault every year. RAINN further reports there is one report of child abuse every ten seconds. Five children that are abused die daily. Three out of five of those children are under four years of age. [6]

This barely scratches the surface of dysfunction, but it gives us an idea of how rampant dysfunction is in America. Once this is understood, it ushers in an understanding of the gross insecurity and fear that taints our society, causing a need to bring a sense of order to our upside down worlds through controlling.

Chapter Two

The Trap of Control

Controllers know no bounds. They can be in church structures, in the work place, or in our own homes. Those bound by control desire to control everyone under their authority and usually for personal purpose and gain. Whether a marriage, the ministry, an interpersonal relationship or in a work relationship, personalities seek to dominate and intimidate their victims, bringing them under their power, position, and influence. Leaders of nations are known to do this. Great examples are Hitler or Stalin. Dictatorships especially, seek control of the people under their leadership.

These controlling personalities are all around us. We frequently see married individuals seeking the consent and advice of a parent, often a mother. A daughter or son may become so dependent on this parent for advice it will become almost impossible to do anything without the parent's consent. The mother may go so far as to tell them everything to do and not to do, right down to raising the children. Even though the mother is not physically in their home with her daughter or son, she controls them.

Married couples are to submit to one another. Instead the interfering parent runs the show or the marriage, causing constant friction and problems for the couple. We hear so many derogatory comments about in-laws. I believe this is one of the reasons why.

Men with controlling mothers get married and are more concerned with what Mama thinks than what their own wives think. Their mothers literally run their lives. Mama always has the last word. What she says goes and unfortunately her word often takes precedence over his wife's word. It creates innumerable problems for her son's marriage. She is quickly labeled the "Monster-in-law."

Many times she drives a wedge between her son and daughter-in-law, or vice versa, resulting in separation or divorce. The "leaving" and "cleaving" principle in Matthew 19:5 is essential for a healthy marriage. A man is to leave his father and mother and cleave to his wife so THEY can become ONE with one another. Mama needs to be put in her place.

Any time a parent gets into the center of a grown child's marriage, it creates problems. Those that fall into patterns of unhealthy control usually do so blindly. That's why it is considered a trap. It becomes a way of life and a habit that seems normal. Most of the time, it is a result of growing up in gross dysfunction or being allowed to control and manipulate others from a young age without intervention. Only by the revelation of the precious Holy Spirit will we come to see our problem of controlling others or being controlled.

The following scenarios paint a picture of control. As you read through each scenario, perhaps they will bring to mind individuals in your life that have controlled you. Maybe you will recognize yourself. Whatever the case, unhealthy control and manipulation is rampant and working all around us.

"Judy's such a control freak. She's always micromanaging every single thing I do. She calls me ten times a day when she's out of the office. I'm perfectly capable of doing my job without all of the interruptions. She's the one who hired me. If she were so worried about whether or not I could do my job, why did she hire me? Being around Judy is suffocating."

"There he goes again. Whenever I tick Seth off, he won't talk to me for a week. He makes me feel like a lowly worm for not agreeing with everything he says. It's *his* way or the highway! I always find myself apologizing when I disagree with him because I can't stand the silence between us. If I tell him I am wrong, even when I know I'm not, it at least breaks the ice."

"Mom is always pulling the same old stunts. When I told her we couldn't spend Christmas with her and Dad this year, she had a conniption fit and started her usual whining and crying, telling me I don't love her, making me feel guilty like she always does. I did what I always do. I gave in and let her have her way. I'm just trying to keep a little peace in the family. After all, *when mama ain't happy, ain't nobody happy.*"

Many of us have been controllers or suffered needlessly at the hands of one. It's no fun. In fact, it will snuff the very life right out of you! The following poem entitled The Demon of Control, I wrote in 2008 after publishing this book the first time, and it is the direct result of my experience involving being a controller and being controlled. Once again, a marvelous picture is painted of the controller:

THE DEMON OF CONTROL

Allow them to control you
Give them everything they seek
Appease them, patronize them,
Continue being weak

Do whatever they tell you
Don't you dare disagree
For if you do, you know the outcome
You'll pay on bended knee

Angry words will slice the air
You'll wish you'd gone along
For choosing to confront
They'll make you feel you're wrong

They'll quickly wield a sword
Of condemnation, guilt, and shame
Then they'll turn on you abruptly
And weave a web of blame

Filled with deep insecurities
And massive levels of fear

They must control their worlds
Holding tightly to what is dear

They'll make demands on everyone
On their beaten path
Handing you a list of expectations
Now, you get to do the math

You'll be expected to do it all
Just as they command it
And if you don't, be assured
They'll throw a bloody fit

When you choose to take a stand
For what you feel is right
You just might get the silent treatment
Till you tell them they were right

For there is but one they seek to please
Only one they must satisfy
Their selfish undertaking
Is for Me, Myself, and I

© Carole McDuffee 2008

There are numerous reasons people fall into the habit of control. Most are completely understandable. Let's start with the definition of a dysfunctional family. Though I cannot remember where I read this particular definition, I thought it was worth sharing:

Dysfunctional Family: A family relationship in which the relationships between the parents and children are strained and unnatural. This is usually because one of the family members has a serious problem—possibly an addiction, that impacts every member of the family. All in this unit feel constrained to adapt atypical roles within the family allowing each family member to survive and function.

We will examine several contributing factors and causes of control, but let's start with the roots: <u>Massive **Insecurity** and **Fear**</u>!

Insecurity: Insecure is defined in the Webster's New Collegiate Dictionary as: Not confident or sure; not adequately guarded or sustained; unsafe; not firmly fastened or fixed; shaky; not highly stable or well adjusted; deficient in assurance; beset by fear and anxiety. [1]

When a child grows up in a dysfunctional home with an unhealthy environment, insecurities develop, which create massive fear.

Fear: An unpleasant often strong emotion caused by anticipation or awareness of danger; anxious concern; reason for alarm; painful agitation in the presence or anticipation of danger. 2

When fear is prevalent within the heart of a man, it often culminates into the habit of control.

Control: To exercise restraining or directing influence over; regulate; to have power over; rule; a personality or spirit believed to actuate the utterances or performances of a spiritualist medium. 3

Let me also highlight some synonyms of control in the Rodale Press, *Synonym Finder,* which does an amazing job of defining control:

Dictate, govern, command, have it all one's way, call the shots, call the plays, run the show; boss, lay down the law, hold the purse strings; wear the pants or the trousers, be in a position of authority; hold all the cards, have the whip hand; wield the scepter, bend to one's will; overpower, domineer, gain the upper hand, get the better of; browbeat, intimidate, bully, ride roughshod over, ride herd on; oppress, repress, suppress, rule with a high hand, rule with an iron hand, rule with a rod of iron, tyrannize; keep down or under, lord it over, break, humble, crush, reduce to slavery, hold captive, hold in bondage; restrict, fetter, shackle; confine, limit, cramp, hamper, encumber, deter, nip in the bud, and put the kibosh on. [4]

These definitions are precisely why I want to address control and the unhealthy habits involved. As I said earlier, control will snuff the life right out of you as is evidenced above!

Control isn't always used in a negative context as it is also defined as: Power or authority to guide or manage. [5] Those in different forms of leadership, for example, will exercise control over a group of people in a business or in a team meeting, but hopefully not in an overly aggressive sense. There must be some sense of control and order in a meeting or else there would be mayhem and disorder. With that in mind, by putting the three definitions together, we might deduce the following definition:

Controller: An individual raised in an unsafe, shaky, unstable home environment. Their home is normally characterized by a deficiency of assurance and security, causing fear, anxiety and insecurity in their personal lives. This results in the habitual exercise of unhealthy restraint or directing influence over a person or persons.

Though there are other reasons individuals learn to control which will be addressed later in this book, I believe there is overwhelming evidence that the majority of controllers are driven by fear and insecurity, some-whether they are raised in a dysfunctional home or not.

    I read a book several years ago by Josh McDowell in which he stated that well over ninety percent of us come from dysfunctional home environments. Most experts in this field agree. Keep in mind that if there is anyone in your home that suffers from an addiction of any kind, whether to drugs, alcohol, gambling, television, food, video games and so on, this qualifies as dysfunction. The level of dysfunction within the home will determine the severity of the control that may be operating as a result.

    There is only one thing to be deducted from a percentage this high: Our society is made up of a massive amount of both children and adults that have become controllers as a result of growing up in dysfunction. I can't begin to wager how many times I've heard various people say in reference to a family member or someone else they know, "So-n-so is a control freak." How many of you know this isn't a positive connotation?

    Let's take a moment and look at a few synonyms for "Freak": Quirk, aberration, anomaly, abnormality, irregularity; monster, monstrosity, idiosyncrasy, peculiarity; mutant, unnatural and malformation. [6]

It is neither normal nor healthy to be a "Control Freak." If you are accustomed to being controlled, it's not fun. It is down right suffocating. If you are a controller, you live in constant turmoil. Peace is not in the picture in either case. Read on. Relief is on the way. Jesus is our deliverer and if you want freedom and you're willing to surrender, you are reading the right book at the right time. For the child of God, there are no coincidences.

Are you ready to rock-n-roll? Okay, then. Put on your Holy Spirit thinking cap and away we'll go! In the next chapter we will delve into the heart of a person who blindly grows into the habit of controlling others.

Chapter 3

A Closer Look at the Insecure Heart

Bitter Root Bitter Judgments

When an individual lives in a dysfunctional home environment, it causes feelings of instability and a lack of control. To bring a sense of security to their upside down worlds, controllers begin taking steps to secure their surroundings through controlling others. When a child or adult has suffered victimization in any form, many times they develop unforgiveness and become bitter with the individual that victimized them. It is not uncommon for them to begin making strong judgments called "bitter root judgments."

A bitter root judgment is a judgment made that begins with the statement: "I will never…or never again will I…" [1]

It is unlikely that a single one of us have escaped making this type of judgment. If you have ever experienced some level of hurt and disappointment in your life, it is quite probable that you have. Think back to a time in your life when you were deeply hurt or experienced disappointment with someone. I made judgments regarding my mother and father's alcoholism: "When I get married and have children, "*I will never* put my children through what my parents are putting me through." A child that grows up with a physically or verbally abusive parent may say, "*Never again* will I allow an adult to hurt me or speak to me in this way. "When I have children, *I will never* lay a hand on them." Out of grave hurt and disappointment with the parent or adult that abused them, they make a judgment against their parent. At that time, a spirit of rebellion may enter them without their personal knowledge which manifests in a number of ways. It all started with a heart filled with pain and anger that culminated in bitterness causing them to declare: "*I will never…*"

Though this is understandable and even normal, it is the bitterness attached to the judgment that causes a problem. In addition, it is not uncommon for the victim to erect a protective wall in conjunction with their "I will never" statement, and a dogged determination that says, "*I dare you to cross over that boundary again. Just try!*" This is a protection mechanism in operation for our safe keeping. As stated previously, a problem arises when anger and bitterness is allowed to grow in our hearts producing a spirit of rebellion.

Though it is a noble desire to want to do better than our parents did, if that desire is accompanied by a bitter root judgment, there will be an unpleasant consequence in the heart of the one who harbors it. Hebrews 12:15 tells us of this peril: "See to it that no one falls short of the grace of God and that no root of bitterness grows up to cause trouble, and defile many."

The Bible tells us that judgment has a reciprocal effect: "Do not judge, or you too will be judged. For in the same way you judge others, you will be judged, and with the measure you use, it will be measured to you (Matthew 7:1-2). Ouch!

John and Mark Sanford in their book <u>Deliverance and Inner Healing</u>, explain this concept well: "We can rightly judge a friend's driving ability by riding in his or her car, but when we judge a parent with an impure heart, we are dishonoring them: When we judge others with impure hearts —with blame, condemnation, anger, envy, jealousy or rancor —then God's immutable laws are set in motion to bring recompense. To judge a parent with an impure heart is to dishonor, and both laws are activated. Our judgment will be meted back to us, and life will not go well with us." [2]

When Control Becomes Witchcraft

Furthermore, when we operate in control out of a place of judgment, there is always the danger of it degenerating into witchcraft. In his book, <u>Confronting Jezebel,</u> Steve Sampson warns us: "Two things have always plagued the Church—control and the desire to dominate. This power struggle has always divided and short-circuited the power of the Church. The desire to control and dominate, if not mastered, can lead to witchcraft, since witchcraft is nothing more than illegitimately controlling the will of another person. The reason the desire to control is akin to witchcraft is that it is in total contradiction to the nature of God Himself. The irrevocable gift God gave to mankind is that of a free will. God Himself refuses to violate His gift of our free will. He will woo us, draw us and attempt to lead us, but He will always leave it up to us to choose His way: I call heaven and earth as witnesses today against you, that I have set before you life and death, blessing and cursing; therefore, choose life that both you and your descendants may live" (Deuteronomy 30:19). [3]

False Responsibility and Role Reversals

When substance abuse, like drugs or alcohol are prevalent in a home, observing a loved one frequently out of control often instills a desire to compensate for inadequacies in the addicted. This can garner a need to become overly responsible, causing one to develop what I call, False Responsibility. Though the need may be one of dire necessity, this dynamic introduces a continuous cycle of unbearable pressure on its victim, causing an inward struggle that produces striving and the need to be overly responsible. Inwardly, a child, (no matter what age), may rationalize, *I need to take care of mom or dad. After all, they aren't able to take care of him/herself. If I don't do this, who will? Because mom is drunk most of the time or dad is high on drugs, someone needs to be responsible.*

In this case, another dynamic sets the stage: Role Reversal. Role Reversal comes into play when a child becomes a care giver to the parent because the parent is unable to care for themselves. If there are small children in the home, in the same way we may reason within, *I need to step in and take care of the children. Someone needs to see that their needs are met.* When a child has to repeatedly shoulder such responsibilities at a young age, it produces incredible insecurity within them. The younger the child, the greater the insecurity.

The inadequacy felt often causes them to feel "Out of Control." This causes them to attempt to compensate for their gross insecurity by striving to control situations and people. And the cycle continues. This is part of becoming codependent.

Though we will only touch lightly on what it is to be codependent, I have recommended some books to further educate yourself on the subject below.

Codependency

The codependent individual seeks to cover up the behavior of the alcoholic or drug addict by making excuses for his or her behavior. Covering up for them enables the negative behavior in the addict to continue. This is a sure way for the addict to never obtain help. For instance, if the codependent individual knows where the hidden stash of drugs or alcohol is, he or she may attempt to *control* the addict's abuse by flushing the drugs down the toilet or pouring the alcohol out. This is an effort to keep them from taking more drugs or drinking more alcohol. The codependent person may end up becoming obsessed with the behavior of the alcoholic searching the bars in town for their loved one, or making phone calls to try to locate them.

First of all, someone who is addicted to drugs or alcohol will always find a way to get more. The attempt to protect the addicted or *control* substance abuse normally fails. Secondly, hunting the individual down in person or by phone will only serve to produce guilt, shame and anger in them when caught in the act of consumption. This rarely produces fruit. Instead, it is likely to produce frustration. These are just a few examples of codependent behavior.

For a greater understanding of codependency, I strongly recommend that you read Melody Beattie's books, Codependent No More, Codependent's Guide to the Twelve Steps, and Beyond Codependency. Even though I am uncertain Melody is a Christian, I do know that the Holy Spirit led me to these books and used them to begin breaking codependency off of me. (We must not limit God in the avenue He chooses to heal and deliver us from unhealthy habits). If He can use a donkey like the one that spoke to Balaam in Numbers 6:21-30, He can also use those that are not Christians.

The Down Fall of Abuse

Because physical and verbal abuse is often rampant in homes where drug or alcohol abuse is prevalent, the level of dysfunction and insecurity leading to a need to control others only increases. Repeated put downs from a parent or a care giver, or even from another adult in our lives, causes a deep wounding of the spirit which requires healing.

Physical abuse is likewise as destructive. Over time, both will cause fear and insecurity to begin to grow in the heart of its victim. Without supernatural intervention, this will produce a need to control others to secure their worlds. Whether there is continual victimization through repeated abuse, the trickle-down effect of the addictive life style of a parent or a spouse, or some other form of dysfunction, it will almost always culminate in the need to control.

Repeated abuse in a child or adult's life can also cause an imbalance in disciplining their own children. It is not uncommon to see parents that were abused as children going to the opposite extreme in discipline. Driven by a fear of being like their abusive parent, they withhold discipline from their children altogether, blindly causing insecurity in their children's hearts, as well as creating rebellion and discipline issues.

As I alluded earlier, wounded individuals surround themselves with self-made walls of protection. Rather than helping themselves, their desperate need to control their world with self-made protection, finds them quickly plummeting into a downward spiral of stagnancy, never arriving anywhere. Their attempt to keep some degree of normalcy in their world backfires. Sadly, these walls even prevent the Healer Himself, from helping them.

Controller's Are Rarely Flexible

Controllers learn to manipulate circumstances according to their wants and desires and are rarely flexible. They will do whatever is necessary to bring their sense of order to their world. They will whine, cry, and throw fits heaping guilt on those who disrupt their "picture perfect plan." When they succeed in controlling and making others do what they want them to do on a consistent basis, they begin developing a false security in their ability to control, and their lust for power increases. If they are not confronted concerning their behavior, they will continue in this anxiety-producing habit of destruction, never finding the peace that they so desperately need.

Controllers Must Rule the Roost

Controllers are notorious for being hard to live with when they are confronted. It is not uncommon for them to become angry at the one who confronts them. The level of anger is in direct proportion to the strength of the stronghold operating. In their minds, they must protect their right to control at all costs. Most of us have probably heard the expression "walking on egg shells." That's exactly what it's like living with a controller. It's a world of chaos. Those who live with the controller live in fear of making them angry. They know if they don't go along with everything the controller says, all hell will break loose and they will pay the consequences for choosing to do otherwise.

How many times have you heard someone say, "Whatever you do, don't say anything to Mrs. (C)ontroller about… (You fill in the blank.) If you do, crap is going to hit the fan." Living in this type of environment produces incredible bondage. This is where the expression "walking on egg shells" comes from. Living with a controller requires extreme care and having to tip-toe carefully around so we do not upset them. I'm sure you've heard the phraseology: "I'm damned if I do and damned if I don't." With a controller, there will be times that no matter what you do, they won't be happy. The only level of peace to be had is when Mr. or Mrs. "C" is being placated and their feathers aren't ruffled. What about this slang expression? "If Mama ain't happy, ain't nobody happy!" Well, if Mr. or Mrs. "C" isn't happy, the same applies. Everyone within a hundred mile radius will know about it.

Those who thrive on being in control might plan a family or work activity to suit their own selfish desires, rather than planning an activity suited to all who are involved. Then the expectation is for everyone around them to succumb willingly to the plan. God forbid if anyone decides not to go along with what the controller has organized. If you choose not to participate even for legitimate reasons beyond your control, you will hear about it for weeks on end or may become the victim of the "silent treatment."

Because control is a mechanism that controllers use to bring security and certainty to their worlds, they are not overly concerned with the cost involved to others who are caught up in their web of control. To them, it is a life and death situation. They see their constant intervention as beneficial and even necessary.

Occasionally, this can be caused by feelings of superiority, believing that others are incapable of handling matters properly or the fear that things will go wrong if they don't attend to every detail. In extreme cases, they simply enjoy the feeling of power that control gives them.

Bull Dog Tenacity

Have you ever seen somebody swing a bull dog around on a rope or drag him to and fro? The dog will latch onto that rope and with dogged determination will not let go. It is very similar with controllers. They will latch onto whatever they are controlling and they will not let go. Laden with massive fear and insecurity, they cannot imagine not controlling their circumstances. Their sense of being in control, is the very thing that makes their world manageable and secure.

Control, Manipulation, & Rebellion

Control, manipulation, and rebellion work together simultaneously. As we mentioned earlier, control can very often become witchcraft if one is not careful. Author, Steve Sampson in his book, Confronting Jezebel says, "Witchcraft, which is a work of the flesh (see Galatians 5:20), manifests in three ways—manipulation, intimidation and domination. Witchcraft is illegitimate authority!" [4]

1 Samuel 15:23 leaves no question that the desire to control others must be dealt with. There is a fine line between rebellion, manipulation, and control. The scripture says, "Rebellion is as the sin of witchcraft." Those who control others are standing on the fringes of opening themselves up to a spirit of witchcraft. Now *that* is scary. I have to believe, the majority of us would not knowingly subject ourselves to the bondage that witchcraft entails. If the *fear of the Lord* is not kicking in right about now, maybe we need to ask ourselves "Why?"

World renowned author and speaker, Derek Prince, reinforces Sampson's sentiments by saying that the root of witchcraft lies in the flesh, which manifests in manipulation, intimidation and domination. Additionally, in his book, They Shall Expel Demons, he says this of control: "The goal is domination. People who recognize that they are weaker than those they seek to control tend to manipulate; those who feel stronger tend to intimidate. But the end purpose is the same: To dominate—that is, to control others and get them to do what we want." 5

Controllers have a difficult time trusting God to take control of their lives by giving up the driver's seat of their Cadillac. They have a death grip on their steering wheel in what is called "the old white knuckle approach." They have made up their minds to be the pilot and the co-pilot, and to dictate to every passenger how and what they should do during the ride.

They are so accustomed to "being in charge" that surrendering to Christ as Lord of their lives becomes a foreign concept. It often causes a sense of panic in the beginning of their relationship with Jesus, which is perfectly normal. Praise the Lord, He is patient and long-suffering, and willing to teach each one of us surrender one step at a time. We must be open and teachable. The continual faithfulness of the Lord will eventually win us over, producing security within.

I think we have clearly established that dysfunction of every kind, including that of sexual abuse, physical and verbal abuse, and other addictions, promote an insecure home environment, producing fear and insecurity. Living with someone who abuses substances of any kind or who is involved in some type of habitual sin that has become addictive, will always produce gross insecurity and fear in those who live with them, whether they show it or repress it.

Please make special notations in this book or a notebook regarding insecurities that you have seen in yourself or others, causing you to operate in control.

Chapter Four

Multiplicity in the Valley of Control

The Island of Guilt

Guilt trip, anyone? I am not talking about touring the Hawaiian Islands here. You won't find one ounce of relaxation visiting the Island of Guilt. Pretty Hawaiian girls will not meet you with a Lei of flowers when you make your way off of the plane into the airport. There won't be a Luau and a banquet table lavished with delectable and luscious fruits native to the island, gentle Hawaiian music, and a few beautiful girls doing the hula.

Unfortunately a trip to this island leaves us wanting… wanting to get on the first flight out. Guilt, shame and condemnation are not the least bit entertaining, but instead, they are three of the devil's biggest tools to keep God's children in bondage. He drops the bomb on us as subtly or as blatantly as the vehicle he chooses to use, and many times without any notice. When it's detonated, there's a gray cloud that settles down over us and a brick that attaches itself to our shoulders. If this isn't recognized, it could be carried for weeks, months, or years on end. It is discharged subtly with as little as a few words, no words (the silent treatment), or blatantly being read the riot act.

Here is a classic scenario where the tool of manipulation is used, which always results in guilt: A mother may say to her son who is spending an exorbitant amount of time at his girlfriend's home: "When are you going to spend time at home? If you really loved me, you would spend some time here, too. You know, one day *I will be dead and gone and you are going to regret the fact that you didn't care. I guess I'm not important to you.*" Can anyone say, "Guilt trip?" This mother's son may need to be spending more time at home, but mama is going about it all wrong. The Bible says that condemnation is not from God: "Therefore there is now no condemnation for those who are in Christ Jesus" (Romans 8:1). Just for the record, neither is putting guilt or shame on another when they don't do what we want. In this case, this mother's steeping her son in condemnation will probably have the opposite effect on him, causing him to avoid her altogether. Do you know anybody that wants to bask in that kind of oppression? Seriously?

Have you ever been on the phone with a controller and disagreed with something they said when they decided to pull the ever popular, hanging-up-on-you act? There you are holding your phone with a blank stare on your face, mumbling in disbelief "What did I say?" To your chagrin, you have just entered the "Island of Guilt" like I mentioned earlier: One big-fat-guilt trip. Most of us have been there. These trips are not a whole lot of fun, and relaxation isn't a part of the picture. You won't enjoy yourself. You will instead, be steeped in oppression. The black cloud of guilt will drop on you like a cold-wet blanket making you feel horrible, unless you recognize it and take authority over it.

Master Manipulators

Little girls, and even little boys, are master manipulators. They learn at an early age how to turn on the charm until their little spigots drip 100% pure cane sugar. Their sticky little fingers can turn mommy and daddy's head anyway they choose. Any amount of money in daddy's pocket becomes his little darling's with enough, "Please Daddies?" He's wrapped around her little finger and she knows it! She milks it for all it's worth. What she wants, she gets! After all, she's "Daddy's Little Girl!" This is where the term to "Sweet Talk" came into being. She will sweet talk her Daddy until she gets exactly what she wants. Unfortunately, Daddy's succumbing to every little whim because of her manipulation, is not only spoiling her, he is doing her a far greater injustice than that. He is creating a monster. She will grow up, get married, and do the same thing to her husband and children unless this unhealthy pattern of control is cut off and severed from her life.

    Many grandparents love to spoil their grandchildren and send them home to mom and dad. Some live for the day when they will have grandchildren to spoil. Whatever the situation, we must make it a priority to be conscious of what we are doing so as not to produce an unhealthy internal control on the inside of them.

    If we are without grandchildren, we would do well to ponder the dangers here, so when the day comes, we won't be guilty of creating a manipulator. When we take our children, grandchildren, or a niece or a nephew with us to a store, are they hounding us for toys and candy every single time we step foot into Walmart, Target, or a similar store? We should be conscious of their ploy to try to get their own way, even in the store. One sure test to know whether or not we are treading into dangerous territory with our little darling(s) is this: While in a store, wait for them to ask for candy or a toy and then lovingly but firmly tell them "No, not this time." After telling them no, if they throw a fit in the middle of the store, or begin hounding us, guess what? You may have a problem on your hands that will have to be dealt with. You may be contributing to creating a monster. A child should be able to go to the store with you without having to have a toy or candy every time they go. If you succumb to their every whim and desire in the name of love, it may end up not being love at all. It may propagate blatant manipulation and that is not showing love.

How many of us have experienced children or teenagers that beg and plead to do something when we have already said "No?" "What part of "No" do you not understand?" "The N or the O?" And yet, with enough doors slamming, screaming and crying, pleading and whining, we say, "Alright, Alright! Go! Get out of my hair. I don't want to hear it any more. I have had enough!" They run out the door and we let out a sigh of relief. "At last, some peace," we mutter to ourselves as we settle into our easy chair! Little do we realize, our problems have just escalated! We have just opened up a huge can of worms that will have to be reckoned with. This same scenario will probably be repeated over and over.

Chapter Five

Blatant Forms of Control

Turning on the Spigot of Tears

Tears can be a great tool used to manipulate. Though girls seem to use this weapon more than boys because of the difference in emotional make up, boys are not immune. Both will use tears and temper tantrums to get their own way. If not nipped in the bud at an early age, this unhealthy habit will be carried into their adult lives.

While my husband and I lived in San Diego, our first naval duty station, I whipped across a four lane highway in a few seconds rather than changing lanes one at a time. I looked in my rear view mirror and low and behold, here came the flashing red lights. My heart dropped into my stomach as it palpitated profusely and my knees turned to jelly. (You know the feeling…) The tears kicked in instantly as I pulled over to the side of the road. When I rolled down my window, the soft hearted officer took one look at me after asking to see my driver's license and proof of insurance and said, "I'm just going to give you a warning this time." After regaining consciousness from a near nervous break down and my heart beat returning to normal, I took a mental note: *Hmmmm, the crying must have helped. He only gave me a warning!*

The next time I was stopped for pulling out of my bank's parking lot into oncoming traffic in what I felt was plenty of time, I found the officer who stopped me to be in disagreement with that theory. Turning on the tears didn't seem to work this time. Bam! Busted! And, thank God I was. It broke at least part of the controlling spirit that was operating in me through manipulation.

Idle Threats

Parents also use idle and even unrealistic threats to control their children. You will find threats most often start with "If you don't" or "If you aren't": "If you don't clean your room TODAY I am going to ground you. If you aren't home by 10:00 p.m., you will have extra chores tomorrow."

I know plenty of parents that have been guilty of this, including me. Idle threats are nothing more than control tactics if you do not follow through. Your kids will get your number very quickly and learn that your threats are nothing more than *empty promises*. They will keep doing what they have always done and change will not come into their lives, at least not from what we are teaching them. It will be business as usual as they think, *Mom and Dad never follow through with what they say. Why should I do what they are asking?*

Money Manipulators

We've all heard the phrase "Money talks." Some people are easily manipulated through threats to withdraw financial support from an organization or an individual. It is not uncommon for church members to manipulate their Pastor(s) with money: "If you don't do things *my way*, I am going to leave the church and take my tithes and offerings else where." Sad to say, many Pastors are guilty of people pleasing and allowing this form of manipulation to control their decision making. Once again, by enabling the controller, they are hindering their growth and doing their church body a great disservice, not to mention displaying a lack of trust in God for their provision.

Brandishing "Old Yeller!"

More than one adult has grown accustomed to yelling to get what they want from their children, a mate, or another. Some even use cussing in the process. This fallacy is enforced by a supposition that says, *they will know that I mean business when I raise my voice.* Or will they? The majority of us turn a deaf ear to yelling and we won't hear a single word that is said when victimized by it. It will go in one ear and out the other. We should never have to yell or cuss to get what we want or expect. Shouting is nothing more than blatant manipulation and is often a control tactic implemented when we have grown accustomed to not following through with what we say. Often we feel we must enforce what we want through raising our voices or adding emphasis through cussing to get our point across.

The Instillation of Fear & Guilt

Many utilize fear and guilt to intimidate those they are trying to control. Words spoken in anger, can become so deeply engrained in our hearts and minds, they can be extremely difficult to forget. On occasion, I have heard of individuals saying "If you don't do such-n-such, I will kill myself." Harsh words like this can literally haunt us for years on end, causing an intense paranoia within us. Children especially, internalize harsh words spoken to them and could live in years of fear and bondage of the adults in their lives dying if they don't do what they say.

During a heated argument it is not uncommon for us to say things we do not mean. Here again, cussing may take the stage in a fit of anger. Let's say that a mother and daughter were arguing and the argument escalated into things being said by the daughter that she didn't really mean. Mom might then say, "You will regret what you just said to me one day when I am dead and gone," heaping guilt and condemnation upon her daughter.

Numerous times, I've heard mothers say to their children, "If you really loved me, you would do such-n-such." Many of us are probably guilty of this very thing. This leaves the child tormented. They internalize, *Since I don't want to do this, I guess I really don't love, mom. I must be a horrible child, son, or daughter.* They live a life laden with guilt each time this sword is wielded in their direction.

I once had a rather large gentleman come to a garage sale I was having in Charleston, South Carolina. I was selling a set of antique dishes at a price I felt was reasonable. He was determined to purchase them from me for next to nothing. He continued pestering me and attempting to get me to lower the price. When I declined several times, another couple walked up and where do you think they gravitated? Right to the set of antique dishes! They purchased them on the spot without a word. This man was furious and left in a rage.

He tried to intimidate me by his size and gruff behavior. Because I recognized it, I stood my ground and remained firm concerning the reasonable price I wanted for the dishes. I could have given in and let him have them for the price he wanted to pay, but it was early in the day and I knew I would get what I was asking. Had I allowed him to intimidate me with his anger through the instillation of fear, I would have been enabling him in the destructive pattern of control that was operating in his life.

By now, you have probably thought of a few blatant control tactics that you have seen in operation, whether through you or another. List them on the next page as you think of them:

Blatant Control Tactics I Have Operated In

1._____

2._____

3._____

4._____

5._____

Blatant Control Tactics Others Operate In

1._____

2._____

3._____

4._____

5._____

Chapter Six

Subtle Forms of Control

Faith Without Hints is Dead!

Controlling behaviors aren't always blatant. They may be subtle, as well. We've all heard the scripture in James 2:20: "Faith without works is dead." Would you consider this rendition? "Faith without HINTS is dead?" Here's a good example: Several brothers and sisters are gathered together in a prayer meeting. Sister "So-n-So" turns on the water-works (tears), and begins to pray, "Lord, Jesus, I don't know where our next meal is going to come from. You know how we have been struggling. I thank you for meeting my need, Lord. In Jesus Name, Amen!"

I am not making light of people with needs. We all have needs, but can you see the subtle hint here? If God leads you to tell someone about your need, definitely do it, but make sure you aren't manipulating or controlling your brothers and sisters, or friends and family, through your emotions or by playing on theirs.

Many ministries do this. They play on people's emotions in hopes of getting offerings, especially when they are feeling desperate: "Brothers and Sisters, our ministry is going under. We need your help to stay a float. Go to the phone right now and call. Our operators are standing by. P-l-e-a-s-e send a generous gift now or we will never make it." By the same token, I have seen other ministries that do not manipulate in the least. God knows each and every one of our needs. He delights in meeting the needs of His children. He doesn't need our coercion or manipulation to MAKE things happen. He's a BIG God.

Shhh…! The Silent Treatment

Many, many people have used this tactic. Inwardly, a person who is wielding this form of weaponry for control may be thinking: "What did you just say? I'm not l-i-s-t-e-n-i-n-g! Can't you tell I am ignoring you? Don't talk to me. I'm trying to pretend you don't exist. Are you feeling any pain yet? I will make you pay for not seeing things my way.

It's my way or the highway, remember?! I'll just keep doing what I am doing, and eventually I will probably *guilt* you into doing what I wanted you to do in the first place. It works every time. They'll come crawling here shortly."

A friend of mine whom I will call Mary, has watched her mother Sue, go for literal weeks on end without talking to Mary's father or other members of her family when she gets angry at one of them. It may not be a weapon of mass destruction, but it is very much a weapon, and it is destructive! Have you ever been the lucky recipient of this subtle form of control, or been the one to dish it out? Those who use this for manipulation hope their victims will grow weary of being ignored and do whatever it is they have been wanting. Many times they get exactly what they want. Because of it, they become monstrous manipulators. Every time they get away with it, they add another layer of bricks to the stronghold and the wall of control becomes a little denser.

The Cold Shoulder

A bedfellow of the "silent treatment" is the proverbial "cold shoulder." The person that wields this weapon may talk to you, but you will immediately sense their discontent and judgment of you as you stand there shivering in the icy cold igloo they have constructed through their treatment of you.

Withholding Physical Intimacy

Though it seems exceptionally cruel, many women withhold sex from their husbands as a form of control and punishment. I know of a woman who wasn't a Christian, who would only participate in physical intimacy with her husband for payment. She had reduced herself to a prostitute, making her living by the number of sexual favors she produced. Scripture forbids such an act, whether for a man or woman. It is blatant sin, and nothing more than a subtle form of control: "But since there is so much immorality, each man should have his own wife and each woman her own husband. The husband should fulfill his marital duty to his wife, and likewise the wife to her husband. The wife's body does not belong to her alone but also to her husband. In the same way, the husband's body does not belong to him alone but also to his wife. Do not deprive each other except by mutual consent and for a time, so that you may devote yourselves to prayer. Then come together again so that Satan will not tempt you because of your lack of self-control" (1 Corinthians 7:2-5).

Name Dropping

Here's another form of control that we may not readily recognize. While in a conversation, we casually mention an organization we are a part of, someone we are friends with that have clout and are highly influential, or even a prestigious place that we might live. If we are operating with a spirit of insecurity, name dropping in any form could be a ploy to impress others, simply because we do not feel worthy apart from the mention.

Prophecy

In his book Exposing Spiritual Witchcraft, Jonas Clark reminds us that the prophetic word can also be used to control others: "Personal prophesies can bring great comfort to every believer. Witchcraft, however, views the use of personal prophesy as a means to control and manipulate. Scripture admonishes us to *know those that labor among you"* (1 Thessalonians 5:12).

David witnessed King Saul prophesying under the spirit of divination while at Saul's house: "The next day an evil spirit from God came forcefully upon Saul. He was prophesying in his house, while David was playing the harp, as he usually did. Saul had a spear in his hand and he hurled it, saying to himself, "I'll pin David to the wall" (1 Samuel 18:10).

"Thus Saith the Lord"

Some use the name of the Lord to manipulate, by saying "God said" when God didn't say anything at all: "Therefore," declares the Lord, "I am against the prophets who steal from one another words supposedly from me. Yes," declares the Lord, "I am against the prophets who wag their own tongues and yet declare, 'The Lord declares.' (Jeremiah 23:30:31). Maybe we shouldn't be so quick to attach the Lord's name to something that He might not have said.

Quid Pro Quo

Quid Pro Quo is the same as saying, "I'll scratch your back, if you scratch mine. I'll do for you, but I expect a favor in return." When they need something, they conveniently remind you of the favor they did for you: "By the way....do you remember when I did such-n-such for you? It's my turn." It is simply a favor with strings: Manipulation with a capital "M!"

True friends are there for us when we need them, just as we are there for them when they need us. I am not referring to serving one another. I am talking about serving one another *with strings attached.*

Creating False Soul Ties

The creation of "False Soul Ties" happens when an individual appears to take a great interest in us, for the purpose of selfishly fulfilling their own agenda. They deliberately create a false intimacy to use us in some way, shape, or form. They might even lie to us about something or someone, to cause us to take their side against another person. Whatever the case, their purpose is selfish in nature: To use us for their own end.

Using the Word of God

Many misquote the Word of God or take it out of context to manipulate others. A husband might say to his wife, "God's word says you are to submit to me woman," while completely disregarding the portion of the scripture that follows that admonition telling husbands to love their wives as Christ loves the church (Ephesians 6:22-27). All scripture must be interpreted in context with other scriptures to obtain the fuller meaning.

Praying Soulish Prayers

Praying Soulish Prayers is another means of control. This is simply praying our own selfish will instead of the will of God for a person, which again, is akin to witchcraft. *Lord, please make so-n-so do* (and inserting whatever it is we want them to do) in the prayer. There are certain things we know to be the will of God for all of us. Praying the Promises of God, (scriptures that state God's will for all of His children), over individuals as a general rule is safe, but we must not take the Word of God out of context while we do this.

If we are not sure the prayer we are praying is in accordance with God's will, adding "May Your perfect will be done in this situation Lord," is a safeguard. "Not *my* will but *Yours* be done!"

I am sure you can think of plenty of your own examples of subtle control tactics. They come in many sizes and shapes and are as varied as the controllers themselves.

As you recognize them, add them to the list on the next page as you think of them. May we not be duped into enabling this unhealthy habit in another or operating in it ourselves. Recognizing and pin pointing control tactics is half the battle.

Subtle Control Tactics I Have Operated In

1._____
2._____
3._____
4._____
5._____

Subtle Control Tactics I See Others Operating In

1._____
2._____
3._____
4._____
5._____

Chapter Seven

Are You a Victim of Control?

If you are a victim of control as I alluded to earlier, you know what it's like to "walk on egg shells." If you choose not to give in and do what the controller wants, all hell breaks loose. It seems easier to keep peace by letting them have their way, but doing that is doing them a horrible disservice. You will only be enabling them to continue in their destructive behavior. It's better to endure the blow up(s) and suffer awhile, hopefully helping to deliver them from their misery strewn nightmare, than to allow the behavior to continue for months and years on end, strengthening the stronghold in their lives.

Fear is usually rampant when dealing with someone like this, but we must remember this scripture out of the Amplified Bible in 2 Timothy 1:7: "For God did not give us a spirit of timidity (of cowardice, of craven and cringing and fawning fear), but (He has given us a spirit) of power and of love and of a calm and well-balanced mind *and* discipline *and* self-control." It is not experiencing fear that causes problems. It is allowing the fear to control us. It is the devil working through the controller to hold us in bondage to fear, so that we will live in torment, which will inevitably trip us up (1 John 5:18). We *can* choose not to allow him to control us through controllers.

Noted Author and Speaker, Joyce Meyer in her book Approval Addiction warns us about allowing others to control us: "If you are letting someone control your life—intimidate you, manipulate you, and cause you to do what you know in your heart is not right—then you need to break those controlling powers. It is not God's will for us to be controlled by anybody except His Holy Spirit and even that decision He leaves up to us. God won't even force His will on us, so we certainly should not let anyone else do it. Approval addicts almost always end up being controlled and manipulated by other people. Satan always sends someone along their way who is a "user." A user is someone who deviously takes advantage of people for his/her own benefit without any concern for others." [1]

What to do – What to do?

So, what do you do if you realize that you are a victim of control and you want to break out of this unhealthy cycle in which you have become entangled? I am not going to lie to you. This is the hard part. However, the Bible is clear that if we ask *anything* according to the *will of God*, it will be done (John 5:14). He promises us He *will* divinely enable us to do whatever we need to do, in accordance with His will, when we *ASK*. He also tells us we can do *ALL* things through His strength (Philippians 4:13).

When you determine not to allow the controllers in your life to control you because you want to stop enabling them, get ready for a battle. Remember this: In the long run, if you cower, the battle will continue to increase in strength making both you AND the controller miserable for a longer period of time. Since when does ignoring a problem make it magically disappear? It won't. The very same problem will be staring you in the face tomorrow, the next day, and the next.

1. Your number one battle strategy is prayer. Ask the Holy Spirit for a plan and strategy for your particular situation. Do what He reveals to you to do. Since He knows the individual controlling you better than you do, you cannot go wrong by following His lead. *(He will not lead you

to confront someone if He knows that the situation may turn volatile endangering your life or the life of others).

2. When you find yourself right smack dab in the center of a controlling escapade and you are being coerced into doing something you know you can't or don't think you should do, with the boldness and the strength of the Lord enabling you, say: "I'm sorry, I won't be able to do such and such, that date doesn't work for me," or you say whatever you need to say.   Say it assertively and do it in love, but be FIRM.

3. Brace yourself, fully clad in the armor of God for protection (Ephesians 6:10-18), and let them get angry. Realize the greater their control issue, the angrier they will probably become. Remember that God has not given you a spirit of fear (2 Timothy 1:7). It is His desire that you walk in faith, exercising His fearlessness and boldness.

4. Stand your ground. Whatever you do, DO NOT GIVE IN! If you allow the controller to manipulate you through whining, tears, yelling, cussing and putting a guilt trip on you, and you give in, you have accomplished NOTHING. Each time you confront will get easier. Picture a helium balloon. Each time you choose not to give in to the controller, you will be releasing some of the helium that has given the balloon (them) strength to continue in their

shenanigans. Each and every time you confront, the problem will diminish and the balloon (the issue) will get smaller.

5. Finally, continue in prayer for the controller so that they will realize their unhealthy habit and desire complete freedom. Eventually, when Mr. or Mrs. "C" get the message that they cannot control you, they will give up, change dance partners, and do the Controller's Waltz with someone that does not have a clue. Prayerfully, they will eventually realize how unhealthy controlling and manipulating others is and will submit their habit to God altogether. The sooner they surrender all to God, the better for them and for us.

There are myriads of tactics that controllers use to control and manipulate. I am sure you have thought of a few of your own examples while you were reading some of the examples sited here. Maybe you've already listed them in the sections provided. It would be nearly impossible to list them all, but hopefully I have given you some food for thought. My greatest desire is to help you in your journey to be set free from the spirit of control, and to eliminate every one of control's cohorts whether you are the victim of control or the one that is doing the victimizing. In the next chapter we will address what can be done if you recognize yourself as a controller.

Chapter Eight

So I'm a Controller: What Do I Do Now?

If you have a problem controlling others, I am sure that you have recognized that attempting to control our own lives or that of others is a near impossible feat. When you don't succeed at controlling, frustration often ensues making us literal basket cases, ridden with anxiety. A controller has come to believe a supposition that says, "If I don't control my world, my life will spin precariously out of control, and I won't know what to do." Controlling others is a carnal and fleshly act that must be crucified. It is trying to get something from someone else through our own means to satisfy our own desires and selfishness. It transgresses that which is healthy and ultimately causes us to experience unending turmoil, defeat, and unrest in our spirits.

Frank Sinatra sang a song in 1969 entitled, "I Did it My Way." When we do things our way there are consequences, and one of them is misery. God tells us not to trust in the arm of our own flesh. Our flesh will fail us time and time again. The scripture admonishes us instead, to put our trust in God: "Blessed is the man who trusts in the Lord, whose confidence is in Him. He will be like a tree planted by the waters, that sends out its roots by the stream. It does not fear when heat comes. He will dwell in the parched places of the desert in a year of drought and never fail to bear fruit" (Jeremiah 17:7-8). Furthermore, Proverbs 3:5-6 tells us that if we will trust in the Lord with all of our hearts and lean not on our own understanding, acknowledging Him, He will direct our paths.

You can trust God, even if you have experienced a life of great insecurity, fear, and upheaval. He has promised He never leaves nor forsakes his children (Hebrew 13:5). He loves each one of us with an undying love and will never do anything to harm us. It is God's desire that each one of his children find peace and rest in His gentle embrace through the release of a need to control. If we choose to surrender the control of our lives and our need to control others, it will be our first step towards experiencing an amazing peace. It may take time to pull this stronghold down, but it will happen if we set ourselves in agreement with God and His word and obey His direction.

The Word of God is one of the most powerful tools that we will ever have as Christians. As we meditate on it, it will literally transform us (Romans 12:1-2). For instance, if we were to meditate on Psalm 91 until it became heart knowledge, causing it to sink deep within our spirits, would it enable us to trust and to have faith in God? You bet it would! Faith comes by hearing and hearing by the Word of God (Romans 10:17).

The more we read, hear, decree, declare, and meditate on the Word of God, the more our faith is built up. Coupled with God's continued faithfulness in our individual lives, we will grow to believe in a God that can be trusted.

Part of becoming a Christian is making Him the Lord of our lives. Becoming a Christian and giving him the reigns of our lives to lead, guide, and direct us, go hand in hand.

There's a familiar saying you may have heard: "If He's not Lord *of all*, He's not Lord *at all*." We will never be satisfied living our Christian lives for ourselves or according to our own agendas. The scriptures have a great deal to say about this: "We are not our own, we are bought with a price" (1 Corinthians 6:19-20). Paul said he died daily to his fleshly desires. Control and manipulation need to be put to death just like any other part of our flesh. "I am crucified with Christ: nevertheless I live; yet not I, but Christ that liveth in me: and the life which I now live in the flesh I live by the faith in the Son of God, who loves me, and gave himself for me" (Galatians 2:20-KJV).

Ask God to show you specific instances when you are controlling. He will! As soon as He prompts your heart to a circumstance or person you are controlling, repent and ask for help right then and there. Close the door that you have opened to the spirit of witchcraft and control, and see the freedom of Christ take over in your life. He alone is our deliverer.

God will walk you through your need to control step by step by step until you are totally free. When that time comes, you will experience a peace you never thought possible. Guaranteed! Now, I am not saying, you won't have to guard your heart from falling back into your old habits. You will. As long as we are on this earth, we must walk circumspectly with a spirit of discernment operating in our walks with Christ. We must stay on guard, but remember: When it comes to controlling others, there is one word of extreme importance: SURRENDER! We must be proactive in implementing it into our lives. Let us say to the Lord: "I Surrender All," and then DO it!

I remember reading in one of Benny Hinn's books his take on surrender. He said he prays every day that God would enable him to die daily to his mind, will, emotions and desires and to live after God's mind, will, emotions and desires. We need to practice the same. If we are truly seeking after God daily in prayer and in the reading of His Word, day by day transformation should be taking place in our lives.

Something supernatural happens when we surrender anything to God that is not in accordance with His will for us or is not His timing for us. A simple prayer will do: "God, I don't want to control others any more. I repent. I surrender this destructive and unhealthy habit to you. I ask you to free me from my need to control and heal my heart from the insecurity and fear that lurks within. I want to be whole in you. Help me to trust you with all of my heart."

God gave me a precious vision regarding the act of surrender that I want to share with you in the next and final chapter. I think it will bless you.

Chapter Nine

Sweet Surrender

Have you ever asked for something from the Lord that you later found out was not His will for you after all? Or, maybe it was His will but the timing was not right. 1 John 5:14 tells us that if we ask anything according to His will, it will be done for us, no ifs, ands, or buts about it. What do we do when we have been deceived into thinking something is God's will, purpose, and plan for our lives, but we find out that it is nothing more than our own desire or want? We, as children of God, must learn to live lives of complete surrender, regarding everything in our lives, both big and small.

I remember vividly driving down the road one day, pouring my heart out to the Lord about something that I was certain was His will for my life. I had obsessed about this situation for weeks on end and I had convinced myself that this particular thing *was* God's will. I definitely wasn't open to the possibility of it not being what God had ordained for me. I was filled with massive anxiety because it was not coming to pass.

Without realizing it, I was trying to control both the situation and God and I had not one ounce of peace. None! The fact that I didn't have peace should have served as a confirmation that this wasn't from the hand of the Lord, but I can be dense sometimes. Some of us just have thicker skulls than others!

God was desperately trying to bring me to a place of surrender. While He didn't blatantly say, "Carole, this is not my will for your life," He did say, "Carole, I want you to surrender this to me." All at once, He showed me a crystal-clear vision that I will never forget: I saw two fists tightly clinched. I then saw them open up with palms pointed heavenward and I heard the Lord say, "This is how I want you to live, Carole: Holding on loosely to everything in your life, with your palms opened towards heaven. If you do this, I can take from you what is not my will for your life with simple ease. In the same way, I can place in your hands what IS my will." In obedience to the Lord, with tear filled eyes, I said "I surrender this situation to you. I only want your will. Please take this from me." Then, He said something to me that completely took me by surprise. He said, "I can't. You are holding on too tightly."

You see, surrendering in prayer is one thing. Actually releasing whatever it is, is quite another thing. But, we have to start some where! God did eventually have His way. Over a period of a few weeks, I completely released the situation. From that point on, I had a peace I had not yet experienced. So, it may take awhile, but don't give up in releasing to the Lord whatever you need to! It will happen.

Once again, it is absolutely vital to live a life of surrender and to remain pliable and submitted to God's will, even in regards to those things we think are God's will and yet might not be. None of us are immune to being deceived. Our own desires often cloud our ability to discern the will of God.

So often we say, "I surrender this thing to you Lord," but we are found holding onto things and people with tightly clinched fists and hearts that will not let go because we have spent weeks and weeks obsessing about something that is not a part of God's plan for us. We pray carnal, soulish prayers according to our wants and desires, rather than going before the Lord and saying, "God, you know the desires of my heart. This is what I would like, but if this is not a part of your plan and purpose for me, remove this desire from me. I know that your will is perfect and that it is far more perfect than anything I could ever want or desire for myself."

A short time ago, God awakened me with a precious word of knowledge for someone in regards to a situation in which they were trying to control someone. This is the perfect example of what I am trying to relay to you. It was a word about "Release." He said, "Tell them to release this situation and their desire to me and repent for trying to control and manipulate, which is the sin of witchcraft. They have been holding on so tightly to what they want, I am not free to move in their situation." Once again, I saw the vision of the tightly clinched fists and then the palms opening up and pointing heavenward. Imagine that?! When we are trying to control a situation or person, we can actually block God's ability to move in the situation. He will never move against our wills, and will actually sit idly by observing us without intervention, until we reach the end of ourselves and surrender whatever it is to Him.

We will never have the PEACE that the Lord desires to give us when what we want is not a part of God's plan for us. Controlling others or enabling a controller is not God's will for us. Whether your need to surrender involves control or something else, give it to God. Give it in its entirety to the Master and leave it completely up to Him. Could it be that He has something far better for you than what you have wanted for yourself? Is it possible the thing that you have been praying for IS God's will, but the timing is not right? Could He be building your faith in the duration of your wait? Could He be working in your character to enable you to sustain what you are asking for?

God alone holds the answer and the key to fulfilling our desires, but they must be in perfect alignment with His desires. Surrender your need to control to the Savior, for His will is PERFECT.

In the year 1896, Judson W. Van DeVenter wrote the song "I Surrender All" and Winfield S. Weeden put the music to it. I'm sure you will recognize it. If you know the tune, sing it gently to Jesus. Sing it with sincerity of heart, and as many times as you have to, until you trust Him with everything that is within you:

All to Jesus I surrender
All to Him I freely give;
I will ever love and trust Him,
In his presence daily live.
I surrender all, I surrender all;
All to thee, my blessed Savior,

I surrender all.
All to Jesus I surrender,
Humbly at His feet I bow,
Worldly pleasures all forsaken,
Take me Jesus, take me now.
I surrender all, I surrender all;
All to thee, my blessed Savior,
I surrender all.

Surrender should be a daily thing. It will never be a one time thing for any of us. Remember: Paul died daily to his flesh (1 Corinthians 15:31). He knew the secret to becoming more like Christ. We must do the same.

Each time you catch yourself trying to manipulate someone through the use of emotions, or you realize through the gentle nudging of the Holy Spirit that you are operating in control, stop, pray and surrender. If God doesn't control us and allows each one of us to freely choose, so should we allow others to choose what to do, even if it is not in agreement with what we think or feel they should do.

Make a conscious effort to operate in love instead of fear and insecurity. God never uses fear to motivate us. He motivates us through love, and we should do the same for others. The Bible says that love covers a multitude of sins (1 Peter 4:8). It is love that transforms and love that holds the key to changing lives. We will never change anyone through controlling them. We should pray and leave the rest to God. He is the only one that can truly change anyone.

If you should realize someone is operating in control towards you, don't enable them by allowing it. Lovingly but firmly, stand up to them. Then leave the consequences of their actions to God. By doing this, you are helping them to find freedom, while at the same time operating in a healthy manner.

Remember: God has not given you a spirit of fear, but of power and of love and of a sound mind (2 Timothy 1:7), and you can do *all* things through Christ who strengthens you (Philippians 4:13).

The choice to be free from control and to help free others is yours and yours alone. Let me close with this admonition from the Lord out of Deuteronomy 30:19-20: "This day I call heaven and earth as witnesses against you that I have set before you life and death, blessings and curses. Now choose life, so that you and your children may live and that you may love the Lord your God, listen to His voice, and hold fast to him. For the Lord is your life and he will give you many years in the land he swore to your fathers, Abraham, Isaac and Jacob."

As you continue on your journey with our Lord and Savior, Jesus Christ, may you be richly blessed by the heart of a Father that loves each one of us too much to allow us to stay the way we are.

In Christ's Love & Sincere Admonition,

Carole McDuffee

Scriptures to Aid You in Your Quest for Freedom from the Chaos of Controlling:

Anxiety & Fear

Philippians 4:4-7

Do not be anxious about anything, but in everything, by prayer and petition, with thanksgiving, present your requests to God. And the peace of God which transcends all understanding will guard your hearts and your minds in Christ Jesus.

Isaiah 41:10

So do not fear, for I am with you; do not be dismayed, for I am your God. I will strengthen you and help you; I will uphold you with my righteous right hand.

2 Timothy 1:7

For God did not give us a spirit of timidity, but a spirit of power, of love and of self discipline.

1 Peter 5:7

Cast all your anxiety on him because he cares for you.

Luke 12:25-26

Who of you by worrying can add a single hour to his life? Since you cannot do this very little thing, why do you worry about the rest?

Matthew 6:25-34

Therefore I tell, do not worry about your life, what you will eat or drink; or about your body, what you will wear. Is not life more important than food, and the body more important than clothes? Look at the birds of the air; they do not sow or reap or store away in barns, and yet your heavenly Father feeds them. Are you not much more valuable than they? Who of you by worrying can add a single hour to his life? And why do you worry about clothes? See how the lilies of the field grow. They do not labor or spin. Yet I tell you that not even Solomon in all of his splendor was dressed like one of these. If that is how God clothes the grass of the field, which is here today and tomorrow is thrown into the fire, will he not much more clothe you, Oh you of little faith? So do not worry, saying, 'What shall we eat?' or 'What shall we drink?' or 'What shall we wear?' For the pagans run after all these things, and your heavenly Father knows that you need them. But seek first his kingdom and his righteousness, and all these things will be given to you as well. Therefore do not worry about tomorrow, for tomorrow will worry about itself. Each day has enough trouble of its own.

Psalm 27:1

The Lord is my Light and my Salvation--whom shall I fear or dread? The Lord is the Refuge and Stronghold of my life--of whom shall I be afraid?

Ephesians 3:12

In whom, because of our faith in Him, we dare to have the boldness (courage and confidence) of free access (an unreserved approach to God with freedom and without fear). (AMP)

Psalm 27:14

Wait and hope for and expect the Lord; be brave and of good courage and let your heart be stout and enduring. Yes, wait for and hope for and expect the Lord.

Isaiah 35:4

Say to those who are of a fearful and hasty heart, be strong, fear not! Behold, your God will come with vengeance; with the recompense of God He will come and save you.

Isaiah 41:10

Fear not [there is nothing to fear], for I am with you; do not look around you in terror and be dismayed, for I am your God. I will strengthen and harden you to difficulties, yes, I will help you; yes, I will hold you up and retain you with my [victorious] right hand of rightness and justice. (AMP)

Isaiah 41:13

For I the Lord your God hold your right hand; I am the Lord, Who says to you, Fear not; I will help you!

Proverbs 12:25

An anxious heart weighs a man down, but a kind word cheers him up.

Psalm 55:22

Cast your cares on the LORD and he will sustain you; he will never let the righteous fall.

Psalm 94:19

When anxiety was great within me, your consolation brought joy to my soul.

Psalm 139:23-24

Search me, 0 God, and know my heart; test me and know my anxious thoughts. See if there is any offensive way in me, and lead me in the way everlasting.

Ecclesiastes 7:14

A man cannot discover anything about his future.

Trust

Proverbs 3:5-6

Trust in the Lord with all your heart and lean not on your own understanding; in all your ways acknowledge him, and he will make your paths straight.

Psalm 28:7

The Lord is my strength and my shield; my heart trusts in him, and I am helped. My heart leaps for joy and I will give thanks to him in song.

Psalm 111:7

The works of his hands are faithful and just; all his precepts are trustworthy.

Psalm 9:10

Those who know your name will trust in you, for you,
Lord, have never forsaken those who seek you.

Psalm 91

1 He who dwells in the shelter of the Most High
   will rest in the shadow of the Almighty.

2 I will say of the LORD, "He is my refuge and my fortress,
   my God, in whom I trust."

3 Surely he will save you from the fowler's snare
   and from the deadly pestilence.

4 He will cover you with his feathers,
   and under his wings you will find refuge;
   his faithfulness will be your shield and rampart.

5 You will not fear the terror of night,
   nor the arrow that flies by day,

6 nor the pestilence that stalks in the darkness,
   nor the plague that destroys at midday.

7 A thousand may fall at your side,
   ten thousand at your right hand,
   but it will not come near you.

8 You will only observe with your eyes
   and see the punishment of the wicked.

9 If you make the Most High your dwelling—
even the LORD, who is my refuge-

10 then no harm will befall you;
no disaster will come near your tent.

11 For he will command his angels concerning you
to guard you in all your ways;

12 they will lift you up in their hands,
so that you will not strike your foot against a stone.

13 You will tread upon the lion and the cobra;
you will trample the great lion and the serpent.

14 "Because he loves me," says the LORD, "I will rescue him;
I will protect him, for he acknowledges my name.

15 He will call upon me, and I will answer him;
I will be with him in trouble,
I will deliver him and honor him.

16 With long life will I satisfy him
and show him my salvation.

Psalm 22:4-5

In You our fathers put their trust; they trusted and you delivered them. They cried to you and were saved; in you they trusted and were not disappointed.

Psalm 20:6-8

Now I know that the Lord saves his anointed; he answers him from his holy heaven with the saving power of his right hand. Some trust in chariots and some in horses, but we trust in the name of the Lord our God. They are brought to their knees and fall, but we rise up and stand firm.

Psalm 28:7

The Lord is my strength and my shield; my heart trusts in him, and I am helped. My heart leaps for joy and I will give thanks to him in song.

Psalm 22:8

He trusts in the Lord; let the Lord rescue him. Let him deliver him, since he delights in him.

Psalm 62:8

Trust in him at all times, Oh people; pour out your hearts to him, for God is our refuge.

Psalm 118:8

It is better to take refuge in the Lord than to trust in man.

Proverbs 29:25

Fear of man will prove to be a snare, but whoever trusts in the Lord is kept safe.

Nahum 1:7

The Lord is good, a refuge in times of trouble. He cares for those who trust in him.

Psalm 56:4

In God, whose word I praise, in God I trust; I will not be afraid. What can mortal man do to me?

Psalm 56:11

In God I trust; I will not be afraid. What can man do to me?

Isaiah 12:2

Surely God is my salvation; I will trust and not be afraid. The Lord, is my strength and my song; he has become my salvation.

Psalm 37:5-6

Commit your way to the Lord; trust in him and he will do this: He will make your righteousness shine like the dawn.

Proverbs 16:20

Whoever gives heed to instruction prospers, and blessed is he who trusts in the Lord.

Jeremiah 17:7-8

But blessed is the man who trusts in the Lord, whose confidence is in him. He will be like a tree planted by the water that sends out its roots by the stream. It does not fear when heat comes; its leaves are always green. It has no worries in a year of drought and never fails to bear fruit.

Security

Romans 5:13

May the God of hope fill you with all joy and peace as you trust in him, so that you may overflow with hope by the power of the Holy Spirit.

Matthew 7: 24-27

Anyone who listens to my teaching and obeys me is wise like a person who builds a house on solid rock. Though the rain comes in torrents and the flood waters rise and the winds beat against that house it won't collapse, because it is built on the rock. But anyone who hears my teaching and ignores it is foolish, like a person who bills a house on sand. When the rains and floods come and the winds beat against that house, it will fall with a mighty crash.

Psalms 40: 1-2

"I waited patiently for the Lord to help me, and he turned to me and heard my cry. He lifted me out of the mud and

the mire. He set my feet on solid ground and steadied
me as I walked along."

(What God's word is telling us here is that in the changing
and unstable world that we live in, our faith & trust has
to be in Him and Him alone. If we build our lives
on trust in God, we will have a solid foundation that won't
crack under the world's pressure).

Philippians 4:6-7

Do not be anxious about anything, but in everything, by
prayer and petition, with thanksgiving, present your requests
to God. And the peace of God which transcends all
understanding, will guard your hearts and your minds in
Christ Jesus.

(Tell God what you need, and thank him for all he has done.
If you do this, you will experience God's peace, which is far
more wonderful than the human mind can understand.)

Romans 8:31-39

What, then, shall we say in response to this? If God is for us,
who can be against us? He who did not spare his own Son,

but gave him up for us all—how will He not also, along with him, graciously give us all things? Who will bring any charge against those whom God has chosen: It is God who justifies. Who is he that condemns? Christ Jesus, who died —more than that, who was raised to life—is at the right hand of God and is also interceding for us. Who shall separate us from the love of Christ? Shall trouble or hardship or persecution or famine of nakedness or danger or sword?

No, in all these things we are more than conquerors through him who loved us. For I am convinced that neither death nor life, neither angels nor demons, neither the present nor the future, nor any powers, neither height nor depth, nor anything else in all creation, will be able to separate us from the love of God that is in Christ Jesus our Lord.

> (These scriptures tell us two things: (1) Our greatest security comes from knowing the peace of God through prayer. (2) There is nothing that can separate us from God's love).

Healing

Psalm 34:18

The LORD is close to the brokenhearted and saves those who are crushed in spirit.

Isaiah 25:8

The Sovereign LORD will wipe away the tears from all faces.

Psalm 147:3

He heals the brokenhearted and binds up their wounds.

Isaiah 53:4

Surely he took up our infirmities and carried our sorrows.

Psalm 119:28

My soul is weary with sorrow; strengthen me according to your word.

Ecclesiastes 7:2

Death is the destiny of every man; the living should take this to heart.

I Thessalonians 4:13

Brothers, we do not want you to be ignorant about those who fall asleep, or to grieve like the rest of men, who have no hope.

1 Thessalonians 4:14

We believe that Jesus died and rose again and so we believe that God will bring with Jesus those who have fallen asleep in him.

Romans 14:9

For this very reason, Christ died and returned to life so that he might be the Lord of both the dead and the living.

1 Corinthians 15:54

Then the perishable has been clothed with the imperishable, and the mortal with immortality, then the saying that is written will come true: "Death has been swallowed up in victory."

Psalm 43:5

Why are you downcast, 0 my soul? Why so disturbed within me? Put your hope in God, for I will yet praise him, my Savior and my God.

Psalm 112:7

He will have no fear of bad news; his heart is steadfast, trusting in the LORD.

Ecclesiastes 3:1- 4

There is a time for everything, and a season for every activity under heaven: a time to be born and a time to die ... a time to weep and a time to laugh ... a time to mourn and a time to dance...

Luke 6:21

Blessed are you who weep now, for you will laugh.

Psalm 30:11-12

You turned my wailing into dancing; you removed my sackcloth and clothed me with joy, that my heart may sing to you and not be silent.

Proverbs 15:13

A happy heart makes the face cheerful, but heartache crushes the spirit.

Proverbs 17:22

A cheerful heart is good medicine, but a crushed spirit dries up the bones.

Psalm 43:5

Why are you downcast, 0 my soul? Why so disturbed within me? Put your hope in God, for I will yet praise him, my Savior and my God.

Psalm 119:28

My soul is weary with sorrow; strengthen me according to your word.

∾∾∾∾∾∾∾∾∾∾∾∾∾∾∾∾∾∾∾∾∾∾∾∾∾∾∾∾∾
∾∾∾∾∾∾∾∾∾∾∾∾∾∾∾∾∾∾∾∾∾∾∾∾∾∾∾∾∾
∾∾∾∾∾∾∾∾∾∾∾∾∾∾∾∾∾∾∾∾∾∾∾∾∾∾∾∾∾

You, Child of God, are More Than a Conqueror Through Christ That Loves You!

Grab Ahold of the Victory that He Purchased for you at the Cross of Calvary and Don't Let Go Until it Manifests!

∾∾∾∾∾∾∾∾∾∾∾∾∾∾∾∾∾∾∾∾∾∾∾∾∾∾∾∾∾
∾∾∾∾∾∾∾∾∾∾∾∾∾∾∾∾∾∾∾∾∾∾∾∾∾∾∾∾∾
∾∾∾∾∾∾∾∾∾∾∾∾∾∾∾∾∾∾∾∾∾∾∾∾∾∾∾∾∾

End Notes

Introduction

1. Onion News Network, "Dysfunctional Family Statistically Average,"23 June, 2004<http.//www.theonion.com/content/node/32873>.

Chapter One

1. Newton,Michael, TheEncyclopediaofSerialKillers, USA: InfobasePublishing, 2011).

2. U.S. Census 2000.

3. Baker, Jennifer, ForestInstituteofProfessionalPsychology DivorceMagazine,http://www.divorcestatistics.org

4. http://www.compassinterventioncenter.net

5. http://www.ama-assn.org/ama/pub/physician-resources/public-health/promotion-healthy-lifestyles/alcohol-other-drug-abuse.page, American Medical Association.

6. www.rainn.org/statistics Rape Abuse Incest National Network.

Chapter Two

1. Webster's New Collegiate Dictionary, (USA: G & C Merrian Co., 1977), pg. 597.

2. Ibid, pg.419.

3. Ibid, pg. 247.

4. The Synonym Finder, (USA: Rodale Press, 1978), pg. 227.

5. Ibid, pg. 437

Chapter Three

1. Sanford, John & Mark, *Deliverance and Inner Healing,* (Grand Rapids, Michigan: Chosen Books, 1992), pg. 62-68.

2. Ibid, Chapter 3, pg. 57.

3. Sampson, Steve, *Confronting Jezebel,* (Grand Rapids, Michigan: Chosen Books, 2003), Chapter 4, pg. 49.

4. Ibid, pg. 49.

5. Prince, Derek, *They Shall Expel Demons,* (Grand Rapids, Michigan: Chosen Books, 1998), Chapter 15, pg. 137.

Chapter Six

1. Clark, Jonas, Exposing Spiritual Witchcraft, (Hallandale Beach, Florida: Spirit of Life Publishing, 1995), Chapter 3, pg. 52.

Chapter Seven

1. Meyer, Joyce, *Approval Addiction*, (New York, New York: Time Warner Book Group, 2005), Chapter 12, pg. 207.

www.ingramcontent.com/pod-product-compliance
Lightning Source LLC
Chambersburg PA
CBHW060846050426
42453CB00008B/862